INDIAN *Spice* RECIPES

PARRAGON

INDIAN Spice

RECIPES

Exotic Dishes Flavoured with Spices

First published in Great Britain in 1996 by
Parragon Book Service Ltd
Unit 13-17, Avonbridge Trading Estate
Atlantic Road, Avonmouth
Bristol BS11 9QD

ISBN: 0-7525-1972-7

Printed in the United Kingdom

Produced by Kingfisher Design, London

Acknowledgements
Series Design: Pedro Prá-Lopez, Kingfisher Design, London
Designers: Frank Landamore, Frances Prá-Lopez, Kingfisher Design, London
Series Editor: Diana Vowles
Illustrations: Jill Moore
Photography: Iain Bagwell, Martin Brigdale, Amanda Heywood
Home Economists: Jill Eggleton, Nicola Fowler, Cara Hobday
Stylists: Rachel Jukes, Marian Price, Helen Trent

Material contained in this book has previously appeared in
Indian Vegetarian Cooking, Quick & Easy Indian Cooking
and *Classic Indian Cooking*

Note
Cup measurements in this book are for American cups.
Tablespoons are assumed to be 15ml.
Unless otherwise stated, milk is assumed to be full-fat,
eggs are standard size 2 and pepper is freshly ground black pepper

Contents

INTRODUCTION 6

APPETIZERS & SNACKS 10

Minted Onion Bhajis 10
Pakoras 12
Lamb & Tomato Koftas 14
Prawn (Shrimp) Pooris 16

MEAT DISHES 18

Rogan Josh 18
Vindaloo Curry 20
Lamb Biryani 22
Lamb Pasanda 24
Lamb Do Pyaza 26
Lamb Tikka Masala 28
Karahi Chicken 30
Chicken Jalfrezi 32
Tandoori Chicken 34
Shahi Murg 36

FISH & SEAFOOD 38

Green Fish Curry 38
Masala Fried Fish 40
Prawn (Shrimp) Bhuna 42
Curried Crab 44

VEGETABLE DISHES 46

Channa Dal 46
Tarka Dal 48
Aloo Chat 50
Palak Paneer 52
Brindil Bhaji 54

DESSERTS 56

Bananas with Spiced Yogurt 56
Indian Ice-Cream (Kulfi) 58
Sweet Carrot Halva 60
Saffron-spiced Rice Pudding 62

INDEX 64

Indian Cookery

I n recent decades the aromatic warmth and deeply sustaining nature of Indian cuisine have made converts right across the Western world and there can be few people who have never enjoyed the delights of eating a richly fragrant curry. By great good fortune, this type of cookery is not hard to master at home; the complicated techniques and hours of preparation that are required to reproduce the art of French *haute cuisine*, for example, are not needed here.

While it may take a little practice to acquire the knack of producing perfectly cooked rice Indian-fashion the preliminary tries will be quite edible, and spicing, the distinguishing characteristic of this cuisine, is very much a matter of taste – if you choose to add a little more of one spice and cut back on another there is no one who can tell you wrong. While quantities are given for the spices in all the recipes in this book, these are merely guidelines; once you are familiar with the recipes you will begin to feel confident in measuring by eye, nose and experience!

Recurring themes

The herbs and spices that constantly recur in Indian food include fresh coriander (cilantro), garlic, ginger, chilli, cinnamon, cardamom, cayenne pepper, mustard, fenugreek, onion seeds (kalonji), nutmeg, coriander seeds, cumin and turmeric. Of these, the last three are staples, and there are few savoury recipes which do not contain at least one of them.

Coriander (which may be labelled *dhania* in an Asian food store) is native to the Mediterranean region and would have been familiar to the Romans, who were prodigious in their use of spices. It was no

doubt they who introduced it to India when they began trading by sea between India and Egypt in the first century AD. The journey took two years until it was discovered that travelling back and forth in accordance with the southwest and northeast monsoon winds halved the time at sea, greatly increasing opportunities for amassing wealth through trade. It was at this time also that the Silk Road from China first wound its overland route through hazardous terrain, bringing the fabled riches of the Orient to Europe, among them the spices that formed a vital part of early economies. The luxuries the Romans revelled in encompassed jewellery, perfumes, cosmetics and spices from far-flung countries, and in their turn they spread their tastes across the western regions of Europe that came under their sway.

However, with the fall of Rome in the fifth century AD and the descent into the

Dark Ages the trade between East and West dried to a trickle. For about 400 years Europe was largely reliant upon the spices that it was able to grow, and these were accordingly considered to be very important; Emperor Charlemagne (c.742–814) even laid down a decree that some 70 herbs and spices suited to the temperate climate of Europe were to be grown on all the imperial estates. They were also to be found in monasteries, which often had physic gardens where plants of medicinal and culinary value were grown.

So Europe struggled on with blander flavours until the trade with the East was reopened in the 11th century by the Crusades, when once again the exotic aromas from hotter climates permeated the kitchens of the West. Yet it seems that in recent times we largely forgot how to use both these spices and the ones we exported all those centuries ago, for now we buy coriander imported from India and the Middle East.

The Good Spice Guide

A pretty annual plant which can reach about 76 cm/2½ ft with feathery leaves resembling those of flat-leaf (Italian) parsley and tiny pinky-white flowers, coriander *(Coriandrum sativum)* grows best in sun. When the seeds are ripe the plants are harvested in the early morning then dried, threshed and sieved. Cumin *(Cuminum cyminum)* was originally a native of the Nile Valley, though its cultivation spread throughout North Africa and to Asia Minor, Iran, China, India and Indonesia. An annual plant about 30 cm/ 12 inches high with very narrow leaves and sparse pink or white flowers, it is harvested when the seeds turn yellow. In India it is usually dry-roasted before use to bring out its warm, heavy aroma. You may find it in Asian stores under the name of *jeera*.

Turmeric *(Curcuma longa)*, the last of the trio, is nearly always sold ground and is unmistakeable on account of the bright yellow colour which makes it useful as a dye but also a spice to beware of for its capacity to leave stains. It is related to ginger and, as with that plant, it is the rhizome, or root, that is used, the main difference in appearance being that the turmeric root is straighter and slimmer and has bright orange flesh where ginger is off-white. It was one of the most popular spices in ancient Rome, and the 13th-century Venetian explorer Marco Polo, encountering it in China, described it as a useful substitute for saffron – which it still remains, being only a fraction of the price.

India is now the major producer of turmeric, though it is also grown in South America, the West Indies, Indonesia, Vietnam, China, Bangladesh and the Philippines. It is a perennial plant reaching 91 cm/3 ft high, with shiny lance-shaped leaves and insignificant flowers. The whole rhizome is lifted from the ground, and then some is used for propagation purposes while the rest is boiled or steamed before being dried and skinned. It is exported whole, to be then ground and packeted in the consuming country, though you may occasionally find the root in Asian

stores, where it may be sold under the name *haldi.*

When buying ground turmeric, look for a deep colour as this indicates good quality, and buy only small quantities as it quickly loses its flavour. Such is its ubiquity in Indian food, you should have no difficulty in using it up in a short space of time!

Along with cumin and coriander, turmeric is one of the main elements of curry powder and the Indian kitchen would not be complete without it; the combined aroma of these three spices conjures up all the pleasure we associate with a delicious dish from India.

Minted Onion Bhajis

MAKES 12

125 g / 4 oz / 1 cup gram flour
¼ tsp cayenne pepper
¼ – ½ tsp ground coriander
¼ – ½ tsp ground cumin
1 tbsp chopped fresh mint
salt and freshly ground black pepper
4 tbsp strained thick yogurt
65 ml / 2½ fl oz / ¼ cup cold water
1 large onion, peeled, quartered and
    sliced thinly
vegetable oil for frying
sprigs of mint to garnish

1 Put the gram flour into a bowl, add the cayenne pepper, coriander, cumin and mint and season with salt and pepper to taste. Stir in the yogurt, water and sliced onion and mix together well.

2 One-third fill a large, deep frying pan (skillet) with oil and heat until hot. Drop heaped spoonfuls of the flour and onion mixture, a few at a time, into the hot oil and use two forks to neaten the mixture into rough ball-shapes.

3 Fry the bhajis until rich golden brown and cooked through, turning frequently. Drain on paper towels and keep warm while cooking the remainder in the same way. Serve hot or warm, garnished with sprigs of mint.

VARIATION

For a more fiery flavour, add 1 seeded and chopped fresh green chilli to the above ingredients and omit the cayenne pepper, if wished.

Pakoras

SERVES 4–6

125 g / 4 oz broccoli
1 onion
2 potatoes
175 g / 6 oz / 1½ cups gram flour
1 tsp garam masala (see page 30)
1½ tsp salt
½ tsp cayenne pepper
1 tsp cumin seeds
200 ml / 7 fl oz / just under 1 cup water
vegetable oil for deep frying
sprigs of fresh coriander (cilantro) to
*   garnish*

1 Cut the broccoli into small florets, discarding most of the stalk, and cook in a pan of boiling, salted water for 4 minutes. Drain well, return to the pan and shake dry over a low heat for a few moments. Place the broccoli on paper towels to dry completely while preparing the other vegetables.

2 Peel and thinly slice the onion and separate into rings. Peel and thinly slice the potatoes and pat dry.

3 Place the gram flour in a bowl with the garam masala, salt, cayenne pepper and cumin seeds. Make a well in the centre, add the water and mix to form a smooth batter.

4 One-third fill a deep fat fryer or pan with oil and heat to 190°C/375°F or until a cube of day-old bread browns in 30 seconds. Dip the vegetables into the batter to coat, then lower into the hot oil and fry, in batches, for 3–4 minutes or until golden brown and crisp. Drain on paper towels and keep warm while cooking the remainder in the same way. Serve the pakoras hot, garnished with fresh coriander (cilantro) sprigs.

VARIATIONS

Small cauliflower florets, strips of red or green (bell) pepper and slices of courgette (zucchini) are also very good cooked this way. The cauliflower should be par-cooked in the same way as broccoli (see step 1) before dipping in the batter. Use up the leftover broccoli (or cauliflower) stalks in a soup, rice or main course dish.

Lamb & Tomato Koftas

SERVES 4

250 g / 8 oz finely minced (ground)
   lean lamb
1½ onions
1–2 garlic cloves, crushed
1 dried red chilli, chopped finely (optional)
2–3 tsp garam masala (see page 30)
2 tbsp chopped fresh mint
2 tsp lemon juice
salt
2 tbsp vegetable oil
4 small tomatoes, quartered
sprigs of mint to garnish

YOGURT DRESSING:
150 ml / ¼ pint / ⅔ cup strained thick yogurt
5 cm / 2 inch piece cucumber, grated
2 tbsp chopped fresh mint
½ tsp toasted cumin seeds (optional)

1 Place the minced (ground) lamb in a bowl. Finely chop 1 onion and add to the bowl with the garlic and chilli, if using. Stir in the garam masala, mint and lemon juice and season well with salt. Mix the ingredients well together. Divide the mixture in half, then divide each half into 10 equal portions and form each into a small ball. Roll the balls in the oil to coat. Quarter the remaining onion half and separate into layers.

2 Thread 5 of the balls, 4 tomato quarters and some of the onion layers on to each of 4 bamboo or metal skewers. Brush the vegetables with the remaining oil and cook under a hot grill (broiler) for about 10 minutes, turning frequently until they are browned all over and cooked through.

3 Meanwhile, prepare the yogurt dressing. Mix the yogurt with the cucumber, mint and toasted cumin seeds, if using. Garnish the lamb koftas with sprigs of mint and serve hot with the yogurt dressing.

Prawn (Shrimp) Pooris

SERVES 6

POORIS:
60 g / 2 oz / ½ cup plain (all-purpose)
wholemeal (wholewheat) flour
60 g / 2 oz / ½ cup plain (all-purpose)
white flour
1 tbsp ghee or vegetable oil
2 good pinches of salt
75 ml / 2½ fl oz / 5 tbsp hot water

TOPPING:
250 g / 8 oz fresh spinach, washed and
stalks trimmed
4 tbsp ghee or vegetable oil, plus extra oil for
shallow frying
1 onion, chopped
1 garlic clove, crushed
½ –1 tsp minced fresh red chilli
1–1½ tbsp medium curry paste, to taste
250 g / 8 oz canned chopped tomatoes
150 ml / ¼ pint / ⅔ cup coconut milk
250 g / 8 oz peeled tiger prawns (jumbo
shrimp)

1 Put the flours in a bowl and make a well in the centre. Add the ghee or oil, salt and hot water and mix to form a dough. Leave to stand for 1 hour.

2 Cut the spinach crossways into wide strips by making bundles of leaves and slicing with a sharp knife. Heat the ghee or oil in a frying pan, add the onion, garlic, chilli and spinach and cook gently for 4 minutes, shaking the pan and stirring frequently. Add the curry paste, tomatoes and coconut milk and simmer for 10 minutes, stirring occasionally. Remove from the heat, stir in the prawns (shrimp) and season with salt to taste.

3 Knead the dough well on a floured surface, divide into 6 pieces and shape into 6 balls. Roll out each one to a 13 cm/5 inch round. Heat about 2.5 cm/ 1 inch oil in a deep frying pan (skillet) until smoking hot. Take one poori at a time, lower into the hot oil and cook for 10–15 seconds on each side until puffed up and golden. Remove the poori with a slotted spoon, drain on paper towels and keep warm while cooking the remainder.

4 Reheat the prawn (shrimp) mixture, stirring until piping hot. Arrange a poori on each serving plate and spoon the prawn (shrimp) and spinach mixture on to each one. Serve immediately.

Rogan Josh

SERVES 6

2 tbsp ghee
1 kg / 2 lb braising steak, cut into
  2.5 cm / 1 inch cubes
1 onion, chopped finely
3 garlic cloves
2.5 cm / 1 inch piece ginger root, grated
4 fresh red chillies, chopped
4 green cardamom pods
4 cloves
2 tsp coriander seeds
2 tsp cumin seeds
1 tsp paprika
1 tsp salt
1 dried bay leaf
120 ml / 4 fl oz / ½ cup natural yogurt
2.5 cm / 1 inch piece cinnamon stick
150 ml / ¼ pint / ⅔ cup hot water
pepper
¼ tsp garam masala (see page 30)

1 Heat the ghee in a large flameproof casserole and brown the meat in batches. Set aside in a bowl.

2 Add the onion to the ghee and stir over a high heat for 3–4 minutes.

3 Grind together the garlic, ginger, chillies, cardamom, cloves, coriander, cumin, paprika and salt.

4 Add the spice paste and bay leaf to the casserole and stir until fragrant.

5 Return the meat and any juices in the bowl to the casserole and simmer for 2–3 minutes.

6 Stir the yogurt into the casserole, adding it gradually so that the sauce keeps at simmering point.

7 Stir in the cinnamon and hot water, and pepper to taste.

8 Cover and cook in a preheated oven at 180°C/350°F/Gas mark 4 for 1¼ hours, stirring frequently, until the meat is very tender and the sauce is slightly reduced.

9 Discard the cinnamon stick and stir in the garam masala. Remove any surplus oil from the surface of the casserole before serving.

Vindaloo Curry

SERVES 4–6

100 ml / 3½ fl oz / scant ½ cup oil
1 large onion, sliced into half rings
120 ml / 4 fl oz / ½ cup white wine vinegar
300 ml / ½ pint / 1¼ cups water
750 g / 1½ lb boneless pork shoulder, diced
2 tsp cumin seeds
4 dried red chillies
1 tsp black peppercorns
6 green cardamom pods
2.5 cm / 1 inch piece cinnamon stick
1 tsp black mustard seeds
3 cloves
1 tsp fenugreek seeds
2 tbsp ghee
4 garlic cloves, chopped finely
3.5 cm / 1½ inch piece ginger root, chopped finely
1 tbsp ground coriander
2 tomatoes, peeled and chopped
250 g / 8 oz potato, cut into 1 cm / ½ inch cubes
1 tsp light brown sugar
½ tsp ground turmeric
salt

1 Heat the oil in a large saucepan and fry the sliced onion until golden brown. Set aside.

2 Combine 2 tablespoons of the vinegar with 1 tablespoon of the water in a large bowl, add the pork and stir together well. Set aside.

3 In a food processor, mix the onion, cumin, chillies, peppercorns, cardamom, cinnamon, mustard seeds, cloves and fenugreek to a paste. Alternatively, grind the ingredients together in a pestle and mortar. Transfer to a bowl and add the remaining vinegar.

4 Heat the ghee in a frying pan (skillet) or casserole and cook the pork until it is browned on all sides.

5 Stir in the garlic, ginger and coriander until fragrant, then add the tomatoes, potato, brown sugar, turmeric and remaining water. Add salt to taste and bring to the boil. Stir in the spice paste, cover the pan and reduce the heat. Simmer for 1 hour until the pork is tender. Serve with basmati rice and pickles.

Lamb Biryani

SERVES 4

½ tsp salt
250 g / 8 oz / generous 1 cup basmati rice,
    washed and drained
2 garlic cloves
2.5 cm / 1 inch piece ginger root, grated
4 cloves
½ tsp black peppercorns
2 green cardamom pods
1 tsp cumin seeds
1 tsp coriander seeds
2.5 cm / 1 inch piece cinnamon stick
1 tsp saffron strands
50 ml / 2 fl oz / 4 tbsp tepid water
2 tbsp ghee
2 shallots, sliced
¼ tsp grated nutmeg
¼ tsp chilli powder
500 g / 1 lb boneless leg of lamb, cut into
    2.5 cm / 1 inch cubes
180 ml / 6 fl oz / ¾ cup natural yogurt
30 g / 1 oz / 2 tbsp sultanas (golden raisins)
30 g / 1 oz / ¼ cup flaked (slivered)
    almonds, toasted

1 Bring a large saucepan of salted water to the boil. Add the rice and boil for 6 minutes. Drain and set aside.

2 Grind together the garlic, ginger, cloves, peppercorns, cardamom pods, cumin, coriander and cinnamon.

3 Combine the saffron and water and set aside. Heat the ghee in a large saucepan and add the shallots. Fry until golden brown then add the ground spices, nutmeg and chilli powder. Stir for 1 minute and add the lamb. Cook until evenly browned.

4 Stir in the yogurt then add the sultanas (golden raisins). Simmer for 40 minutes, stirring occasionally.

5 Pile the rice on the sauce in a pyramid. Trickle the saffron and soaking water over the rice in lines. Cover the pan with a clean tea towel (dish cloth), put the lid on and cook over a low heat for 10 minutes. Uncover the pan and with a wooden spoon handle make 3 holes in the rice to the level of the sauce but not touching it. Replace the tea towel (dish cloth) and the lid and leave to stand for 5 minutes.

6 Uncover the pan, lightly fork the rice and serve, sprinkled with the almonds.

Lamb Pasanda

SERVES 4

500 g / 1 lb boneless lamb shoulder
150 ml / ¼ pint / ⅔ cup red wine
75 ml / 3 fl oz / ⅓ cup oil
3 garlic cloves, crushed
5 cm / 2 inch piece ginger root, grated
1 tsp ground coriander
1 tsp ground cumin
2 tbsp ghee
1 large onion, chopped
1 tsp garam masala (see page 30)
2 fresh green chillies, halved
300 ml / ½ pint / 1¼ cups natural yogurt
2 tbsp ground almonds
20 whole blanched almonds
salt

1 Cut the lamb into strips of about 2.5 cm/1 inch across and 10 cm/ 4 inches long. Set aside.

2 Combine the red wine, oil, garlic, ginger, coriander and cumin in a large non-metallic bowl. Stir in the lamb and leave to marinate for 1 hour.

3 Heat the ghee in a frying pan (skillet) and fry the onion until brown.

4 Drain the lamb, reserving the contents of the bowl. Pat the lamb dry with paper towels. Add the lamb to the frying pan (skillet) and stir over a high heat until it is evenly sealed and browned.

5 Add the contents of the bowl to the pan and bring to a gentle boil. Add the garam masala, chillies, yogurt, ground almonds, whole almonds, and salt to taste. Cover and simmer for 12–15 minutes until the lamb is tender.

Lamb Do Pyaza

SERVES 4

2 tbsp ghee
2 large onions, sliced finely
4 garlic cloves, 2 of them crushed
750 g / 1½ lb boneless lamb shoulder, cut
    into 2.5 cm / 1 inch cubes
1 tsp chilli powder
2.5 cm / 1 inch piece ginger root, grated
2 fresh green chillies, chopped
½ tsp ground turmeric
½ tsp salt and ground black pepper
180 ml / 6 fl oz / ¾ cup natural yogurt
2 cloves
2.5 cm / 1 inch piece cinnamon stick
300 ml / ½ pint / 1¼ cups water
2 tbsp chopped fresh coriander (cilantro)
3 tbsp lemon juice

1 Heat the ghee in a large saucepan and add 1 of the onions and the garlic. Cook for 2–3 minutes, stirring constantly.

2 Add the lamb and brown all over. Remove and set aside.

3 Add the chilli powder, ginger, chillies and turmeric and stir for a further 30 seconds.

4 Add plenty of salt and pepper, the yogurt, cloves, cinnamon and water. Return the lamb to the pan. Bring to the boil then simmer for 10 minutes.

5 Transfer to an ovenproof dish and place uncovered in a preheated oven at 180°C/350°F/Gas mark 4 for 40 minutes. Check the seasoning.

6 Stir in the remaining onion and cook uncovered for a further 40 minutes.

7 Add the fresh coriander (cilantro) and lemon juice. Serve with naan bread.

Lamb Tikka Masala

SERVES 6

1 tsp ground cumin
½ tsp ground turmeric
5 cm / 2 inch piece ginger root, grated
2 garlic cloves, crushed
½ tsp salt
120 ml / 4 fl oz / ½ cup natural yogurt
1 kg / 2 lb boneless lamb, cut into
   2.5 cm / 1 inch cubes
1–2 drops edible red food colouring
1 tsp water
fresh mint leaves to garnish

MASALA SAUCE:
1 tbsp ghee
3 tomatoes, peeled and chopped
½ tsp yellow mustard seed
2 fresh green chillies, chopped
120 ml / 4 fl oz / ½ cup coconut milk
3 tbsp chopped fresh mint
3 tbsp chopped fresh coriander (cilantro)
salt

1 Combine the cumin, turmeric, ginger, garlic, salt and yogurt in a bowl. Stir in the lamb until evenly coated with the sauce. Dilute the food colouring with the water and add to the bowl, stirring well.

2 Marinate in the refrigerator for 2 hours. Soak 6 wooden skewers in warm water for 15 minutes.

3 Make the masala sauce. Heat the ghee in a large saucepan and add the tomatoes, mustard seed, green chillies and coconut milk. Bring to the boil, then simmer for 20 minutes until the tomatoes have broken down. Stir occasionally.

4 Thread the pieces of lamb on to the skewers. Set on a grill (broiler) pan and cook under a preheated very hot grill for 15–20 minutes, turning occasionally.

5 Stir the mint and fresh coriander (cilantro) into the sauce, and season with salt.

6 Carefully remove the lamb from the skewers. Stir the lamb into the sauce and serve garnished with mint leaves.

Karahi Chicken

SERVES 4–6

2 tbsp ghee
3 garlic cloves, crushed
1 onion, chopped finely
2 tbsp garam masala (see right)
1 tsp ground coriander
½ tsp dried mint
1 dried bay leaf
750 g / 1½ lb boneless chicken meat, diced
200 ml / 7 fl oz / scant 1 cup chicken stock
    or water
1 tbsp finely chopped fresh coriander
    (cilantro)
salt

1 Heat the ghee in a karahi, wok or
large, heavy frying pan (skillet) and
add the garlic and onion. Stir for about
4 minutes until the onion is golden.

2 Stir in the garam masala, ground
coriander, mint and bay leaf.

3 Add the chicken and cook over a high
heat, stirring occasionally, for about
5 minutes.

4 Add the chicken stock or water and
simmer for 10 minutes, until the
sauce has thickened and the chicken
juices run clear when the meat is tested
with a sharp knife.

5 Stir in the fresh coriander (cilantro),
add salt to taste and serve with naan
bread or chapatis.

GARAM MASALA

Garam masala can be bought ready-made in supermarkets and Asian food stores, but you may prefer to make your own. There are many variations on the recipe for garam masala, but this is the one that has been used in this book: grind 1 teaspoon cardamom seeds, 2 teaspoons cloves, 2 tablespoons cumin seeds, 2 tablespoons coriander seeds, 2 dried bay leaves, 7.5 cm / 3 inch piece cinnamon stick, 1 tablespoon black peppercorns and 1 dried red chilli together in a spice grinder, coffee mill or pestle and mortar until the aromas are released. Store in an airtight jar and use as required.

Chicken Jalfrezi

SERVES 4

1 tsp mustard oil
3 tbsp vegetable oil
1 large onion, chopped finely
3 garlic cloves, crushed
1 tbsp tomato purée (paste)
2 tomatoes, peeled and chopped
1 tsp ground turmeric
½ tsp ground cumin
½ tsp ground coriander
½ tsp chilli powder
½ tsp garam masala (see page 30)
1 tsp red wine vinegar
1 small red (bell) pepper, chopped
125 g / 4 oz / 1 cup frozen broad (fava)
   beans
500 g / 1 lb cooked chicken, cut into
   bite-sized pieces
½ tsp salt
sprigs of fresh coriander (cilantro)
   to garnish

1 Heat the mustard oil in a large frying pan (skillet) set over a high heat for about 1 minute until it begins to smoke. Add the vegetable oil, reduce the heat and then add the onion and the garlic. Fry the onion and garlic until they are golden.

2 Add the tomato purée (paste), chopped tomatoes, turmeric, cumin, coriander, chilli powder, garam masala and vinegar to the frying pan (skillet). Stir the mixture until fragrant.

3 Add the red (bell) pepper and broad (fava) beans and stir for 2 minutes until the pepper is softened.

4 Stir in the chicken and add salt to taste. Simmer gently for 6–8 minutes until the chicken is heated through and the beans are tender.

5 Serve garnished with sprigs of fresh coriander (cilantro).

Tandoori Chicken

SERVES 4

8 small chicken portions, skinned
3 dried red chillies
1 tsp salt
2 tsp coriander seeds
2 tbsp lime juice
2 garlic cloves, crushed
2.5 cm / 1 inch piece ginger root, grated
1 clove
2 tsp garam masala (see page 30)
2 tsp chilli powder
½ onion, chopped and rinsed
300 ml / ½ pint / 1¼ cups natural yogurt
1 tbsp chopped fresh coriander (cilantro)
lemon slices to garnish
cucumber raita (see below right) to serve

1 With a sharp knife, make 2–3 slashes in the flesh of each chicken piece.

2 Crush together the chillies, salt, coriander seeds, lime juice, garlic, ginger and clove. Stir in the garam masala and chilli powder. Transfer to a small saucepan and heat gently until aromatic.

3 Remove the pan from the heat and add the onion and yogurt.

4 Arrange the chicken in a non-metallic dish and pour the yogurt mixture over it. Cover and put in the refrigerator to marinate for 4 hours or overnight.

5 Arrange the chicken on a grill (broiler) tray and cook under a preheated very hot grill (broiler) or over a barbecue for 20–30 minutes, turning once, until the chicken juices run clear when the thickest parts of the portions are pierced with a sharp knife.

6 Sprinkle the chicken with chopped fresh coriander (cilantro). Serve hot or cold, garnished with the lemon slices and accompanied by cucumber raita.

CUCUMBER RAITA

Mix together 250 g / 8 oz / 1 cup natural yogurt, 2 tsp chopped fresh mint, 175 g / 6 oz cucumber, peeled, deseeded and cut into matchsticks, and salt to taste. Serve as a cooling accompaniment to any spicy dish.

Shahi Murg

SERVES 4

2 tbsp ghee
1 onion, sliced finely
8 small–medium chicken pieces
1 tsp ground cumin
1 tsp ground coriander
½ tsp salt
350 ml / 12 fl oz / 1½ cups natural yogurt
120 ml / 4 fl oz / ½ cup double (heavy)
   cream
1 tbsp ground almonds
½ tsp garam masala (see page 30)
3 cloves
seeds from 3 green cardamom pods
1 dried bay leaf
60 g / 2 oz / ⅓ cup sultanas (golden raisins)
sprigs of fresh coriander (cilantro)
   to garnish

1 Heat half the ghee in a large saucepan and cook the onion over a medium heat for 15 minutes, stirring occasionally, until the onion is very soft.

2 Meanwhile, heat the remaining ghee in a large frying pan (skillet) and brown the chicken pieces well. Add to the onion.

3 Add the cumin, coriander, salt, yogurt, cream, almonds and garam masala to the onion and chicken.

4 Bring to a gentle simmer and add the cloves, cardamom, bay leaf and sultanas (golden raisins).

5 Simmer for 40 minutes until the chicken juices run clear when the thickest part of each piece is pierced with a sharp knife, and the sauce has reduced and thickened.

6 Serve garnished with sprigs of fresh coriander (cilantro).

Green Fish Curry

SERVES 4

1 tbsp oil
2 spring onions (scallions), sliced
1 tsp cumin seeds, ground
2 fresh green chillies, chopped
1 tsp coriander seeds, ground
4 tbsp chopped fresh coriander (cilantro)
4 tbsp chopped fresh mint
1 tbsp chopped chives
150 ml / ¼ pint / ⅔ cup coconut milk
4 white fish fillets, about 250 g / 8 oz each
salt and pepper
sprigs of mint to garnish

1 Heat the oil in a large frying pan (skillet) or shallow saucepan and add the spring onions (scallions).

2 Stir-fry the spring onions (scallions) over a medium heat until they are softened but not coloured. Stir in the cumin, chillies and ground coriander, and cook them until fragrant.

3 Add the fresh coriander (cilantro), mint, chives and coconut milk and season liberally.

4 Carefully place the fish in the pan and poach for 10–15 minutes until the flesh flakes when tested with a fork.

5 Serve the fish fillets in the sauce, garnished with sprigs of mint and accompanied by basmati rice.

Masala Fried Fish

SERVES 4–8

8 plaice or other white fish fillets, about
    125–150 g / 4–5 oz each
1 tbsp ground turmeric
2 tbsp plain (all-purpose) flour
salt
½ tsp ground black peppercorns
1 tsp chilli powder
1 tbsp ground coriander
1 garlic clove, crushed
2 tsp garam masala (see page 30)
oil for deep frying

TO GARNISH:
lemon wedges
chilli powder

1 To skin the fish fillets, lay the fillet skin-side down with the tail nearest you. Take the tail end between your thumb and forefinger. With your other hand, hold a sharp knife at a shallow angle to the fish. Holding the fish firmly, make an angled cut between the flesh and the skin, then continue to cut the flesh away from the skin until it is free.

2 In a shallow dish, combine the turmeric, flour, salt, peppercorns, chilli powder, coriander, garlic and garam masala. Mix well.

3 Fill a shallow saucepan or a deep frying pan (skillet) with oil to a depth of 5–7.5 cm/2–3 inches, and heat to 180°C/350°F or until a cube of bread browns in 30 seconds.

4 Coat the fish fillets in the spice mix either by shaking gently in a paper bag or turning over in the dish of spice mix until well coated.

5 Deep fry the fish fillets for about 3–5 minutes, turning often until the fish flakes with a fork. Drain on plenty of paper towels.

6 Garnish with lemon wedges and a sprinkling of chilli powder, and serve with a selection of pickles and chutneys.

Prawn (Shrimp) Bhuna

SERVES 4–6

2 dried red chillies, deseeded if liked
3 fresh green chillies, finely chopped
1 tsp ground turmeric
2 tsp white wine vinegar
½ tsp salt
3 garlic cloves, crushed
½ tsp ground black pepper
1 tsp paprika
500 g / 1 lb uncooked peeled tiger prawns
    (jumbo shrimp)
4 tbsp oil
1 onion, chopped very finely
180 ml / 6 fl oz / ¾ cup water
2 tbsp lemon juice
2 tsp garam masala (see page 30)
sprigs of fresh coriander (cilantro)
    to garnish

1 Combine the chillies, turmeric, vinegar, salt, garlic, pepper and paprika in a non-metallic bowl. Stir in the prawns (shrimp) and set aside for 10 minutes.

2 Heat the oil in a large frying pan (skillet) or wok, add the onion and fry for 3–4 minutes until soft.

3 Add the prawns (shrimp) and the contents of the bowl to the pan and stir-fry over a high heat for 2 minutes.

4 Reduce the heat, add the water and boil for 10 minutes, stirring from time to time, until the water is evaporated and the curry is fragrant.

5 Stir the lemon juice and garam masala into the prawn (shrimp) mixture.

6 Serve garnished with sprigs of fresh coriander (cilantro).

Curried Crab

SERVES 4

2 tbsp mustard oil
1 tbsp ghee
1 onion, chopped finely
5 cm / 2 inch piece ginger root, grated
2 garlic cloves
1 tsp ground turmeric
1 tsp salt
1 tsp chilli powder
2 fresh green chillies, chopped
1 tsp paprika
125 g / 4 oz / ½ cup brown crab meat
350 g / 12 oz / 1½ cups white crab meat
250 ml / 8 fl oz / 1 cup natural yogurt
1 tsp garam masala (see page 30)
fresh coriander (cilantro) to garnish

1 Heat the mustard oil in a large, preferably non-stick, frying pan (skillet), wok or saucepan. When it starts to smoke add the ghee and onion. Stir for 3 minutes over a medium heat until the onion is soft.

2 Stir in the grated ginger and the whole garlic cloves.

3 Add the turmeric, salt, chilli powder, chillies and paprika. Stir to mix thoroughly.

4 Increase the heat and add the crab meat and yogurt. Simmer, stirring occasionally, for 10 minutes until the sauce is thickened slightly. Add garam masala to taste.

5 Serve hot over plain basmati rice, with the fresh coriander (cilantro) either chopped or in sprigs.

Channa Dal

SERVES 4–6

2 tbsp ghee
1 large onion, chopped finely
1 garlic clove, crushed
1 tbsp grated ginger root
1 tbsp ground cumin
2 tsp ground coriander
1 dried red chilli
2.5 cm / 1 inch piece cinnamon stick
1 tsp salt
½ tsp ground turmeric
250 g / 8 oz / 1 cup split yellow peas,
   soaked in cold water for 1 hour and
   drained
425 g / 14 oz can plum tomatoes
300 ml / ½ pint / 1¼ cups water
2 tsp garam masala (see page 30)
sprigs of fresh coriander (cilantro)
   to garnish

1 Heat the ghee in a large saucepan, add the onion, garlic and ginger and fry for 3–4 minutes until the onion has softened slightly.

2 Add the cumin, coriander, chilli, cinnamon, salt and turmeric, then stir in the split peas until well mixed.

3 Add the contents of the can of tomatoes, breaking the tomatoes up slightly with the back of the spoon.

4 Add the water and bring to the boil. Reduce the heat to very low and simmer, uncovered, for about 40 minutes, stirring occasionally, until most of the liquid has been absorbed and the split peas are tender. Skim the surface occasionally with a slotted spoon to remove any scum.

5 Gradually stir in the garam masala, tasting after each addition, until the channa dal is of the required flavour. Serve garnished with sprigs of fresh coriander (cilantro).

Tarka Dal

SERVES 4

2 tbsp ghee
2 shallots, sliced
1 tsp yellow mustard seeds
2 garlic cloves, crushed
8 fenugreek seeds
1 cm / ½ inch piece ginger root, grated
½ tsp salt
125 g / 4 oz / ½ cup split red lentils
1 tbsp tomato purée (paste)
600 ml / 1 pint / 2½ cups water
2 tomatoes, peeled and chopped
1 tbsp lemon juice
4 tbsp chopped fresh coriander (cilantro)
½ tsp garam masala (see page 30)
½ tsp chilli powder

1 Heat half of the ghee in a large saucepan and add the shallots. Cook for 2–3 minutes over a high heat, then add the mustard seeds. Cover the pan until the seeds begin to pop.

2 Immediately remove the lid from the pan and add the garlic, fenugreek, ginger and salt.

3 Stir once and add the lentils, tomato purée (paste) and water and simmer gently for 10 minutes.

4 Stir in the tomatoes, lemon juice and fresh coriander (cilantro) and simmer for a further 4–5 minutes until the lentils are tender.

5 Transfer to a serving dish. Heat the remaining ghee in a small saucep until it starts to bubble. Remove from heat and stir in the garam masala and chilli powder. Pour it over the tarka da immediately and serve accompanied b naan bread.

Aloo Chat

*125 g / 4 oz / generous ½ cup chick-peas
(garbanzo beans), soaked overnight in
cold water and drained*
1 dried red chilli
*500 g / 1 lb waxy potatoes, such as red-
skinned or Cyprus potatoes, boiled in their
skins and peeled*
2 tsp salt
1 tsp cumin seeds
1 tsp black peppercorns
½ tsp dried mint
½ tsp chilli powder
½ tsp ground ginger
2 tsp mango powder
120 ml / 4 fl oz / ½ cup natural yogurt
oil for deep frying
4 poppadoms
cucumber raita (see page 34) to serve

1 Boil the chick-peas (garbanzo beans)
with the chilli in plenty of water for
about 1 hour until tender. Drain.

2 Cut the potatoes into 2.5 cm/1 inch
dice and mix into the chick-peas
(garbanzo beans) while they are still
warm. Set aside.

3 Grind together the salt, cumin and
peppercorns in a spice grinder or
pestle and mortar. Stir in the mint, chilli
powder, ginger and mango powder.

4 Put a small dry saucepan or frying
pan (skillet) over a low heat and add
the spice mix. Stir until fragrant and
immediately remove from the heat.

5 Stir half of the spice mix into the
chick-peas (garbanzo beans) and
potatoes, and stir the other half into
the yogurt.

6 Cook the poppadoms according to
the packet instructions. Drain on
plenty of paper towels. Break into bite-size
pieces and stir into the chick-peas
(garbanzo beans) and potatoes, spoon the
spiced yogurt over the top and serve with
the cucumber raita.

Palak Paneer

2 tbsp ghee
1 onion, sliced
1 garlic clove, crushed
1 dried red chilli
1 tsp ground turmeric
salt and pepper
500 g / 1 lb waxy potatoes, such as red-
    skinned or Cyprus potatoes, cut into
    2.5 cm / 1 inch cubes
425 g / 14 oz can tomatoes, drained
150 ml / ¼ pint / ⅔ cup water
250 g / 8 oz / 6 cups fresh spinach
500 g / 1 lb / 2 cups curd cheese, cut into
    2.5 cm / 1 inch cubes
1 tsp garam masala (see page 30)
1 tbsp chopped fresh coriander (cilantro)
1 tbsp chopped fresh parsley

1 Heat the ghee in a saucepan, add the onion and cook over a low heat for 10 minutes until very soft. Add the garlic and dried chilli and cook for a further 5 minutes.

2 Add the turmeric, salt, potato cubes, tomatoes and water to the pan and bring to the boil.

3 Simmer for 10–15 minutes until the potatoes are cooked.

4 Stir in the spinach, cheese cubes, garam masala, fresh coriander (cilantro) and parsley.

5 Simmer for a further 5 minutes and season well with salt and pepper. Serve with naan bread.

Brindil Bhaji

SERVES 4

500 g / 1 lb aubergines (eggplant)
2 tbsp ghee
1 onion, thinly sliced
2 garlic cloves, sliced
2.5 cm / 1 inch piece ginger root, grated
½ tsp ground turmeric
1 dried red chilli
½ tsp salt
425 g / 14 oz can tomatoes
1 tsp garam masala (see page 30)
sprigs of fresh coriander (cilantro)
   to garnish

1 Using a sharp knife, cut the aubergines (eggplant) into 1 cm/½ inch thick rounds then slice the rounds into finger-width strips.

2 Heat the ghee in a saucepan and cook the onion over a medium heat for 7–8 minutes, stirring constantly, until very soft.

3 Add the garlic and aubergine (eggplant), increase the heat and cook for 2 minutes.

4 Stir in the ginger, turmeric, chilli, salt and tomatoes. Use the back of a wooden spoon to break up the tomatoes. Simmer uncovered for 15–20 minutes until the aubergine (eggplant) is very soft.

5 Stir in the garam masala and simmer for a further 4–5 minutes.

6 Serve garnished with sprigs of fresh coriander (cilantro).

Bananas with Spiced Yogurt

SERVES 4–6

3 good pinches saffron strands
2 tbsp creamy milk
6 cardamom pods, split and seeds removed
    and crushed
45 g / 1½ oz / 3 tbsp butter
45 g / 1½ oz / 3 tbsp soft brown sugar
½ tsp ground cinnamon
2 bananas
500 g / 1 lb strained thick yogurt
2–3 tbsp clear honey to taste
30 g / 1 oz / ¼ cup flaked (slivered)
    almonds, toasted

1 Place the saffron strands on a small piece of kitchen foil and toast very lightly. Crush the saffron strands finely and place in a small bowl. Add the milk and crushed cardamom seeds, stir well and leave to cool.

2 Meanwhile, melt the butter in a frying pan (skillet), add the brown sugar and cinnamon and stir well. Peel and slice the bananas and fry gently for about 1 minute, turning halfway through cooking. Remove from the pan and place in decorative serving glasses.

3 Mix the yogurt with the cold spiced milk and honey to taste. Spoon the mixture on top of the bananas and liberally sprinkle the surface of each serving with the toasted almonds. Chill before serving, if preferred.

Indian Ice-Cream (Kulfi)

SERVES 6–8

75 ml / 2½ fl oz / 5 tbsp boiling water
4 cardamom pods, split and seeds removed
405 g / 14 oz can sweetened condensed
  milk
75 ml / 2½ fl oz / 5 tbsp cold water
30 g / 1 oz / ¼ cup unsalted pistachio nuts
30 g / 1 oz / ¼ cup blanched almonds
2 drops almond flavouring (extract)
  (optional)
150 ml / ¼ pint / ⅔ cup double (heavy)
  cream

TO DECORATE:
lime zest
rose petals (optional)

1 Pour the boiling water into a bowl, stir in the cardamom seeds and leave for 15 minutes to infuse. Meanwhile, put the condensed milk into a blender or food processor together with the cold water, pistachio nuts, almonds and almond flavouring (extract), if using. Process the mixture for about 30 seconds until very finely mixed.

2 Add the cooled and strained cardamom water and pour into a bowl. Whip the cream to soft peak stage and whisk into the mixture. Pour the mixture into a shallow metal or plastic container and freeze for about 3 hours or until semi-frozen around the edges and mushy in the centre.

3 Transfer the mixture to a bowl and mash well with a fork to break up the ice crystals. Divide the mixture evenly between 6–8 small moulds and freeze for at least 4 hours or overnight until firm.

4 To serve, dip the base of each mould briefly into hot water and run a knife around the top edge. Turn out on to serving plates and decorate with lime zest and rose petals, if using.

Sweet Carrot Halva

SERVES 6

750 g / 1½ lb carrots, peeled and grated
750 ml / 1¼ pints / 3 cups milk
1 cinnamon stick or piece of cassia bark
  (optional)
4 tbsp vegetable ghee or oil
60 g / 2 oz / ¼ cup granulated sugar
30 g / 1 oz / ¼ cup unsalted pistachio nuts,
  chopped
30–50 g / 1–2 oz / ¼–½ cup blanched
  almonds, slivered or chopped
60 g / 2 oz / ⅓ cup seedless raisins
8 cardamom pods, split and seeds removed
  and crushed
thick cream or yogurt to serve
sprigs of mint to garnish

1 Put the grated carrots, milk and cinnamon or cassia, if using, into a large, heavy-based saucepan and bring to the boil. Reduce the heat to a simmer and cook, uncovered, for 35–40 minutes, or until the mixture is thick, with no milk remaining. Stir the mixture frequently during cooking to prevent it sticking.

2 Discard the cinnamon or cassia. Heat the ghee or oil in a non-stick frying pan (skillet), add the carrot mixture and stir-fry over a medium heat for about 5 minutes or until the carrots take on a glossy sheen.

3 Add the sugar, pistachios, almonds, raisins and cardamom seeds, mix well and continue frying for a further 3–4 minutes, stirring frequently. Serve warm or cold with thick cream or yogurt and a garnish of sprigs of mint.

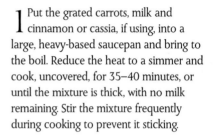

Saffron-spiced Rice Pudding

SERVES 4–5

600 ml / 1 pint / 2½ cups creamy milk
several pinches of saffron strands, finely
*   crushed (see below right)*
60 g / 2 oz / ¼ cup short-grain (pudding)
*   rice*
1 cinnamon stick or piece of cassia bark
45 g / 1½ oz / 3 tbsp granulated sugar
30 g / 1 oz / ¼ cup seedless raisins or
*   sultanas (golden raisins)*
30 g / 1 oz / ¼ cup ready-soaked dried
*   apricots, chopped*
1 egg, beaten
75 ml / 3 fl oz / ⅓ cup single (light) cream
15 g / ½ oz / 1 tbsp butter, diced
15 g / ½ oz / 2 tbsp flaked (slivered)
*   almonds*
freshly grated nutmeg for sprinkling
cream to serve (optional)

1 Place the milk and crushed saffron in a non-stick saucepan and bring to the boil. Stir in the rice and cinnamon or cassia, reduce the heat and simmer very gently, uncovered, for 25 minutes, stirring frequently until tender.

2 Remove the pan from the heat and discard the cinnamon or cassia from the rice mixture. Stir in the sugar, raisins or sultanas (golden raisins) and apricots, then beat in the egg, cream and butter.

3 Preheat the oven to 170°C/325°F/Gas mark 3. Transfer the mixture to a greased ovenproof pie or flan dish and sprinkle with the almonds and freshly grated nutmeg to taste. Cook in the oven for 25–30 minutes until the mixture is set and lightly golden. Serve hot with extra cream, if wished.

SAFFRON

For a slightly stronger saffron flavour, place the saffron strands on a small piece of kitchen foil and toast them lightly under a hot grill (broiler) for a few moments (take care not to overcook them or the flavour will spoil). Crush finely between fingers and thumb before adding to the milk.

Index

A

Aubergine:
Brindil Bhaji 54

B

Bananas with Spiced
Yoghurt 56
Beef:
Rogan Josh 18

C

Carrot:
Sweet Carrot Halva 60
Chicken:
Jalfrezi 32
Karahi 30
Shahi Murg 36
Tandoori 34
Chick-peas:
Aloo Chat 50
Crab, Curried 44

E

Eggplant See Aubergine

F

Fish:
Green Fish Curry 38
Masala Fried Fish 40

G

Garam masala 30
Garbanzo beans
See Chick-peas

I

Ice-cream, Indian (Kulfi) 58

K

Kulfi 58

L

Lamb:
Biryani 22
Do Pyaza 26
Pasanda 24
Tikka Masala 28
& Tomato Koftas 14
Lentils:
Tarka Da 48

P

Pakoras 12
Peas:
Channa Dal 46
Pork:
Vindaloo Curry 20
Potatoes:
Palak Paneer 52

Prawn:
Bhuna 42
Pooris 16

R

Rice Pudding,
Saffron-spiced 62

S

Shrimp See Prawn

V

Vegetables:
Aloo Chat 50
Brindil Bhaji 54
Channa Dal 46
Minted Onion Bhajis 10
Pakoras 12
Palak Paneer 52
Tarka Dal 48